OBVERSE   REVERSE

A NUMISMATIC HISTORY & ANALYSIS: TYPE II DOUBLE EAGLES 1866-1876

FOURTH EDITION

Printed In The United States Of America. The Publisher Takes No Responsibility for The Use By Third Parties Of Any Of The Information, Materials Or Methods Described In This Book, Nor For The Products Described Herein.

FOREWORD

I have both collected and dealt in rare United States gold coins for many years. It is our experience that the best way to begin (or expand) a collection is to be able to read as much as possible. Even with my 40+ years experience in the field of United States gold coins, I find myself continually reading and trying to improve my level of expertise.

I have long been enamored with the Type Two Double Eagle series. I have bought and sold many important Type Two Double Eagles and assembled personal collections. As much as I enjoy this series, I continually complained that there was no reference work to consult.

So I did something that would benefit not only us but the entire numismatic community as a whole: I wrote the very first book exclusively about Type Two Double Eagles.

In this book, I have attempted to share all that I know about these coins. It is my sincere hope that the enthusiasm I feel towards these visually impressive, historically significant gold pieces will be conveyed to you.

As you assemble your set, I urge you to frequently refer to this book. Instead of reading it from cover to cover, look at a specific date entry when you are considering adding this issue to your collection. What you've read should help you better judge the coin which you may or may not buy.

As pricing changes often we encourage you to get updated pricing from your dealer and recognize all pricing in books become outdated over time.

I wish you good luck assembling a set of Type Two Double Eagles and I hope you come to know and enjoy these coins as much as I do!

Mike Fuljenz

TABLE OF CONTENTS

By: Mike Fuljenz

HOW TO UNDERSTAND AND USE THIS BOOK

This book has a standardized format for each of the thirty one Type Two Double Eagles issues. By taking a few minutes to read this chapter, the collector will be better able to understand this book. This will, in turn, make this book more useful and a better tool in assembling a set of coins. Type Two Double Eagles were struck from 1866 until 1876. They were produced at three mints: Philadelphia (1866-1876), San Francisco (1866-1876) and Carson City (1870-1876). The twenty nine basic issues are supplemented by two significant varieties from 1873: the Open and Closed 3's.

Each of these issues is accorded a distinct entry in this book. The entry begins with a photograph of a specific Double Eagle. Most of the coins chosen to illustrate this book are not exceptional quality. Rather, they are the typical quality coins which are generally offered for sale. If a coin you purchase is better than the coin illustrated, it does not necessarily mean that you have a very important coin. All it means is that your coin, at the very least, is better than average.

After the mintage figure for each coin is listed, there are rarity rankings for each issue. These are divided into two distinct classifications: overall rarity and premium quality rarity. Overall rarity refers to the total number of coins which exist for a specific issue. Premium quality refers to the number of coins which exist in About Uncirculated-50 or better grades. Each issue is ranked in relation to the total thirty one coin series and in relation to the issues from each specific mint.

The first paragraph for each issue contains some basic information. This information typically focuses on one or two factors which make an issue interesting or distinctive from others.

The second paragraph contains four basic components regarding every issue: strike, luster, surfaces and coloration. Each Type Two Double Eagle shows a unique and distinctive pattern of strike. Some coins are well struck (i.e., they show much of the detail intended on the original design) while others are poorly struck. This book discusses the typical quality of strike for both the obverse and the reverse of each Type Two Double Eagle. Any peculiarities of strike which occur on a significant number of coins from a specific issue are mentioned. By comparing your coin to the description of strike, you can judge if you have a well struck, average struck or poorly struck coin and whether the value of a specific coin is closer to the upper or lower end of the price range listed for each issue.

The quality of luster for each issue is discussed next. Some Type Two Double Eagles show a frosty texture, others show a satiny texture and still others have a mirror-like or Prooflike finish. This is another opportunity for the collector to compare his coin with what has been most typically observed for each specific issue. When discussing the surfaces of a Type Two Double Eagle, this book is most concerned with abrasions and/or bagmarks. As a rule, this series is found with very heavily abraded surfaces. Other areas which are discussed under the heading of surfaces include such mint-made flaws as copper spotting and planchet faults.

The coloration of Type Two Double Eagles encompasses a broad spectrum of hues and depends primarily on which issue is being examined. This book describes the coloration seen most often on higher grade, uncleaned examples of each specific date. When each of these individual components is added together, a coin can be rated as to its eye appeal. Eye appeal, while somewhat inexact in its description, is what literally makes a coin appealing to the viewer's eye. In the Type Two Double Eagle series, a coin is said to have good eye appeal if it shows a sharp, even strike, minimal abrasions, above-average natural luster and pleasing original coloration. In this book, each Type Two Double Eagle is described in regards to its availability in a high eye appeal state of preservation.

The next paragraph for each issue mentions significant die varieties. For many issues, there are no significant die varieties. For a few others, there are some interesting varieties and these are described.

By: Mike Fuljenz

Philadelphia Type Two Double Eagles had very limited production of Proofs.This book lists the mintage figures for each issue and it gives the approximate number of survivors. The next paragraph is a summary of the rarity of each issue. It states what the typical level of preservation is for each issue and in what grade it becomes uncommon. Mint State rarity levels are accorded separate treatment from circulated grades.

One of the first questions any collector asks about a coin is how rare is it. This book attempts, for the first time, to accurately list the rarity of each Type Two Double Eagle. In the rarity section of each date's entry, the total number of coins estimated to exist is given. This estimate is based on the total number of coins graded by PCGS and NGC, the personal experience of the authors, knowledge of holdings which have not entered the market and auction records. It should be stressed that while these estimates are accurate as to the current coin market,there is always the chance that a hoard could be discovered which could dramatically increase the total population of any date

After listing the overall rarity of each Type Two Double Eagle, a breakdown is given which estimates a coin's rarity in four grade levels: Very Fine, Extremely Fine,About Uncirculated and Mint State. These rarity estimates are ranges. In other words, a certain issue may be estimated to have a surviving population of between 100 and 125 coins in a specific grade. On certain issues, there are population distributions which can cause confusion. For example, it is estimated that 100-150 1875-S Double Eagles exist in Very Fine and 700-800 in Mint State. This does not mean that a Very Fine coin is five to six times more valuable. It means that this was a date that did not circulate freely (like the Carson City issues) and few survivors show extensive wear.

A listing of price levels is given next. These are estimates of retail prices for Type Two Double Eagles based on the current coin market. The low end of the price range is what an average quality coin might sell for while the higher price represents a higher quality coin. Certain very rare issues or exceptionally high grade coins can bring considerably more than the high estimate of these ranges. Each entry concludes with a Condition Census listing. Numismatists define the Condition Census for a date as a listing of the 10 to 15 finest examples and ties of this specific issue. It is very hard to determine an exact Condition Census for most Type Two Double Eagles. This is due to the fact that many dates have too high of a population to formulate an accurate list and others have too many coins of equal quality representing the highest grade range. To compensate for this fact, this book lists what should be an appropriate cut-off point for each date. For example, it is believed that an 1875-S Double Eagle must grade at least Mint State-62 to qualify as a Condition Census example for this specific date.

The author has attempted to make this book informative and as easy to use as possible. While certain information will inevitably become outdated, the basic design and intent of each date by date entry will remain unchanged. If the collector takes a few minutes to understand the intent, this book should prove very useful to him in his attempt to assemble a set of Type Two Double Eagles. But, only the collector can determine what coins, grades and prices suit him.

TYPE TWO DOUBLE EAGLES: A BRIEF HISTORY AND OVERVIEW

One of the principal consequences of the great California gold rush of the late 1840's and the early 1850's was a huge amount of gold bullion coming to the Philadelphia Mint for eventual use as coinage. Suddenly, officials at the Mint had a problem: what would be done with all of this gold.

A solution to this problem lay in the fact that, by this era, the United States had become an international trader of great significance. A large sized gold coin was needed to pay foreign trade debts which were mounting rapidly. The need was made more acute by the fact that a great number of comparable Latin American and South American gold coins were already being used by American merchants to pay off these foreign deficits. Because of this, a bill was passed by Congress in February 1849 which authorized the coining of Twenty Dollar gold pieces which would contain 516 grains of gold.

The task of engraving the new coin fell to Mint Engraver James B. Longacre. His first design employed a bust of Liberty in high relief. This was rejected when Mint officials determined that the coins would not stack. Longacre's second attempt, in the fall of 1849, was also rejected as the dies cracked soon after a few prototypes were struck. His third attempt proved to be successful and a very limited number of Double Eagles dated 1849 were struck in gold. (Only one of these can be traced today and it is impounded in the National Numismatic Collection at the Smithsonian Institute. It is considered to be the most valuable American coin).

Regular production of the Liberty Head Double Eagle began in 1850 at the Philadelphia and New Orleans mints. Longacre's design featured a coroneted Liberty head facing to the right on the obverse with the reverse featuring has an eagle similar to the one found on the Great Seal. The value was abbreviated TWENTY D. This design (known to numismatists as the Type One Liberty Head Double Eagle) continued until 1866.

The Act of March 3, 1865 stated that (where practical) all United States gold coins would have to display the motto IN GOD WE TRUST. James Longacre complied with this request beginning with the coinage of 1866. On the Double Eagle he made some other less obvious changes. This included making the shield on the reverse slightly more ornate, reconfiguring the leaves and slightly elongating the eagle's wing tips and tail feathers.

Today, the United States Double Eagles struck from 1866 through 1876 at the Philadelphia, Carson City (1870-1876) and San Francisco mints are known to numismatists as Type Two Liberty Head Double Eagles. These coins fulfilled the desire of the government to create an important international trade coin. Huge numbers of Type Two Double Eagles were sent overseas to pay foreign trade debts.Others wound up in Europe after ownership was banned in the United States in1933.

For reasons which are still not entirely known, Mint officials decided to change the reverse of the Double Eagle in 1877. These coins, which are known to numismatists as Type Three Liberty Head Double Eagles, feature the value spelled out TWENTY DOLLARS as opposed to TWENTY D. Type Three Double Eagles were struck from 1877 until this type was replaced by the St. Gaudens design in 1907.

The short-lived Type Two Double Eagle series has become very popular with collectors and investors. Only 31 coins are needed to complete the set and all but a small number of these issues can be obtained by the collector of average means.

By: Mike Fuljenz

HOW TO COLLECT TYPE TWO DOUBLE EAGLES

Type Two Double Eagles have proven to be a very popular series with collectors. This is a relatively short-lived group of coins (1866-1876) which consists of only thirty one major issues. With the exception of one of these issues (the 1870-CC; for more information, see below) this is a set which can be completed by a collector of average means.

Type Two Double Eagles appeal to collectors for a number of reasons. They are big, beautiful coins which can be appreciated even by the non-collector. They are plentiful enough that many issues can be found in high grades. However, they are scarce enough that they also appeal to the rarity conscious collector.

There are a number of excellent ways in which to collect Type Two Double Eagles. These range from a casual flirtation with this series to intense devotion. The following listing contains a number of ways to collect these coins. We are aware of a number of collectors who are successfully employing at least one approach.

1. Collecting Type Two Double Eagles As Type Coins. Type coin collectors seek to obtain one representative example of a specific type or design. For Type Two Double Eagles, they would focus on obtaining a common date in the highest grade which they can afford. There are a number of specific dates which they might purchase including the 1873 Open 3, 1875, 1876 and 1876-S. Each of these dates is common enough in grades up to and including Mint State-62 that there is little—if any—date premium.

If you are interested enough in Type Two Double Eagles that you are taking the time to read a book devoted to this series, the chances are good that you will become more involved with these issues than as mere type coins. If you decide to purchase a Type Two Double Eagle strictly as a type coin, it might make sense to pay a small premium and obtain a date which is a bit more rare in higher grades but which sells for a small premium.

2. Collecting Type Two Double Eagles By Mint.

Type Two Double Eagles were produced at three mints: Philadelphia, San Francisco and Carson City. Some collectors are attracted to the issues from just one of these mints and they attempt to put together a complete set of dates and major varieties.

Assembling a complete set of Philadelphia Type Two Double Eagles is not very difficult. There were twelve different major varieties produced in eleven years (in 1873, both Open 3 and Closed 3 varieties exist). In the higher circulated grades, all of these issues can be obtained without great effort. They will range in price from $1300-1600 for the most common dates in About Uncirculated-55 to About Uncirculated-58 up to $12,000 or so for the rarest issues (1868, 1869 and 1870). In Mint State grades, this set can still be assembled but it requires greater patience and deeper pockets. The most difficult issue to locate in Uncirculated grades is the 1868 which may have to be purchased in nice About Uncirculated-58 due to the difficulty of finding a truly Mint State example

A complete set of San Francisco Type Two Double Eagles can also be assembled without great difficulty. As with the Philadelphia coins, there are a total of twelve different varieties struck during eleven consecutive years. In the higher circulated grades, many of these issues can be purchased for less than $3000. In Mint State-60 to Mint State-62 grades, this set becomes extremely challenging. The 1866-S With Motto, 1867-S and 1868-S are all very rare in Uncirculated with current populations of fewer than a couple dozen coins believed to exist.

The Carson City Type Two Double Eagles are the most popular issues with collectors. A total of seven different dates were produced between 1870 and 1876. The great popularity of these coins is contrasted by the extreme difficulty of assembling a complete set. The 1870-CC is easily the rarest Type Two Double Eagle and an acceptable example currently costs in the neighborhood of $200,000-350,000. The 1871-CC is also a rare coin although lower quality pieces can be located. The other Carson City issues can be found in About Uncirculated grades without a great deal of searching. The 1872-CC, 1873-CC and 1874-CC are all rare and expensive in any Mint State grade while very nice examples 1875-CC and the 1876-CC can be found in Mint State.

By: Mike Fuljenz

3. Collecting Type Two Double Eagles By Year. A popular and practical way to collect Type Two Double Eagles is by year. Such a collection would consist of a single example for each year in which the Type Two design was produced. In this case, such a set would have eleven coins.

In a year set, it is advisable to choose the most affordable issue produced in a specific year. For example, an 1870-S Double Eagle would be chosen over an 1870 Philadelphia or an 1870 Carson City since the San Francisco coin is the easiest to obtain in both circulated and Uncirculated grades. The 1870-CC would be the least likely coin to include in this set due to its extreme rarity and very high price.

4. Assembling A Complete Set of Type Two Double Eagles. Many collectors decide to assemble a complete set of Type Two Double Eagles. Such a set will include one example of each Type Two Double Eagle struck between 1866 and 1876. Including both varieties of 1873 and 1873-S, a complete set consists of 31 coins. For the most part, the grades of this set will range from Extremely Fine to Mint State. The more common issues are generally represented by high grade coins while the rare issues are represented by lower grade pieces. The stopper of this set is, of course, the 1870-CC which is very rare and very expensive. However, most of the other Type Two Double Eagles are well within the budget of the average collector.

There are some basic principles which the complete set collector should follow as he acquires coins. A complete set should be as well-matched as possible.The collector should try to purchase coins which have a similar appearance. As an example, a collector might try to acquire coins which are as original as possible and which show reasonably similar coloration.

A complete set should not be all over the map as far as grades are concerned. Instead of spending $3000 on an unappealing, bagmarked 1874-CC (as opposed to a choice example of this date) merely to fill a hole. Do not assemble a complete set with unrealistic expectations. A collector who has previously worked on more common sets may approach Type Two Double Eagles with the idea that he will be able to complete this set in the higher Mint State grades. Since many issues in the Type Two Double Eagle series are essentially non-existent above Mint State-60 (and some like the 1870-CC are unknown in any grade approaching MS-60), certain allowances will have to be made.

Conversely, a collector does not have to settle for coins he does not like just because he thinks he will not be able to do any better.

Set building can be the key to realizing additional value without spending extra money. This phenomenon is known to numismatists as a set premium and it definitely applies to Type Two Double Eagles at certain times. Carefully assembled sets of coins have shown over long years they can bring substantial premiums over randomly assembled,meaningless accumulations of coins.

There are many examples of important sets of United States coins. These include some of the following collections.

- The Garrett family collection was formed by a railroad executive and his sons between the mid 1860s and the late 1930s. After it was donated to Johns Hopkins University, it was sold at auction for more than $25 million in a series of sales held between 1979 and 1981. Many of the prices realized in these sales still have never been broken.

- The Louis Eliasberg collection of United States gold coins was sold at auction in 1982 for over $11 million. This collection was started in the 1940s when Eliasberg purchased the famous John Clapp collection. Eliasberg continued to add to the collection and by the time he died in 1976, he had assembled the single greatest U.S.Gold set ever formed by an individual. Today, coins which are pedigreed to the Eliasberg sale bring a strong premium.

- The Howard Bareford collection was assembled in a seven year period between 1947 and 1954 at a cost of $13,882. In 1978, it was sold at auction for $1,207,215—and it would probably bring multiples of that figure today.

By: Mike Fuljenz

Starting a set of coins is fun and challenging. Finishing a set can be very profitable over a long period of time. And the entire collecting process makes the set building experience worthwhile from start to finish. Perhaps your name will someday be as recognized as Garrett, Eliasberg and Bareford.

An especially good idea for the new collector would be to discuss assembling a set of Type Two Double Eagles with a dealer who specializes in 19th century gold coins. Get his thoughts as to which grade each specific date should be purchased in. Reading this book should also give the collector a good idea about this as it attempts to give a breakdown of the total number known of each date in each grade range.

5. Collecting By Die Variety: For most Type Two Double Eagles, a number of different obverse and reverse dies were employed. As one die became worn and/or damaged, it was replaced by a new die. The different combinations of dies created a number of die varieties.

The field of gold coin die variety collecting is extremely fertile. Very little has been written about the varieties of U.S. Gold coins and next to nothing has been written about the die varieties of Type Two Double Eagles. It is very probable that a number of interesting, potentially rare die varieties exist for this series

A collector wishing to start a die variety collection needs to pay attention to such things as date placement, mintmark placement and diagnostic characteristics such as die scratches. He should record this information and compare each example of a specific date which he has the chance to examine.

While it is possible that this sort of collecting may become popular in the future, for now it is the province of a tiny handful of specialists. Therefore, the die variety collector should not pay an extra premium for supposedly rare varieties (such as a mintmark position previously unseen on a specific issue) with the exception of well-established varieties such as the 1873 Double Die and the 1875 Canceled Obverse Die.

6. Collecting Proof Type Two Double Eagles: Proof Type Two Double Eagles were struck in exceedingly limited quantities at the Philadelphia Mint from 1866 through 1876. In fact, the mintage for Proofs for the entire eleven year period was just 335 pieces.

The tremendous rarity of these coins is what makes them appealing to small segment of wealthy collectors. It is possible to assemble a complete set of Proof Type Two Double Eagles. However, this set would require considerable patience and a very deep pocketbook.

Most of the Proof Type Two Double Eagles which have appeared on the market in the past few years have graded in the Proof-60 to Proof-63 range. The extreme rarity of Proof-64 and better examples makes this set all but impossible to complete in the higher Proof grades.

Before you finish this chapter and start reading about the individual Type Two Double Eagles which interest you, the authors would like to share the irrespective numismatic philosophy. We call it the **Five Ps of rare coin collecting** and we think it can be applied to any series of coins.

> **1. Popularity.** We advise collecting coins that are already popular and are likely to be popular in the future. An already popular coin, like the rare Type Two Double Eagle, figures to be even more popular as time goes on. Newly published books on specific coin series' tend to drives prices higher. For example, in 2001, prices for most $2 1/2 Indian Head Quarter Eagles went **up 50%** in price or more following the release of our award-winning book, **A Collector's Guide to Indian Head Quarter Eagles**. Also, in September 2000, many of our recommended Type III $20 Liberty gold coins **rose in price as much as 100%** in six short months, following the receipt of our first NLG Book of the Year Award, in a specialized category for our book, **Type III Double Eagles: 1877-1907**. Additionally, the sale of the hoard of Type I $20 Liberty gold coins recovered from the S.S. Central America (also accompanied by new books and media attention) created new demand for the already rare Type II $20 Liberties among thousands of new collectors. Over the next couple of years the salvaged gold was marketed to the general public, which seem to drive prices higher. This is like knowing exactly where a new interstate highway is going to be built a couple of years from now. An old economics law states; "Supply creates its

own demand." The sudden increase in the supply of these early "Type I" coins, mostly 1857-S and lesser numbers of 1854-1856 San Francisco $20 Double Eagles, is already creating a dramatic increase in demand for all dates of $20 Liberty Double Eagles series; especially the already rare Type II $20 gold coins. There is no similar hoard of the later, and more rare, Type II coins. So the increase in demand from new collectors is expected to drive Type II prices higher. If collectors wait much longer, they could soon pay higher prices to add the rare Type II $20 Liberty Double Eagles to their collections.

2. Precious Metal. This can be summed up in three words: platinum, gold, or silver. Coins struck in precious metals are more popular and sell more easily than coins struck in copper, nickel or bronze.

3. Pretty. People like coins which are big and pretty better than those which are small and poorly designed. A coin such as the Type Two Liberty Head Double Eagle has a very pleasing design which can be appreciated by the new and veteran collector alike.

4. Preservation. It is always a smart decision to purchase coins in better than average condition. A coin which is above average is much easier to resell in the future and it is more likely to show appreciation than a coin which is only average or below average. In the Type Two Double Eagle series, this is easy to gauge by looking at the rarity estimates in this book.

5. Population: Since the formation of PCGS in 1986 and NGC in 1987, there has been an important body of empirical data developed by the two services. Each services publishes a population report which reveals exactly how many coins have been graded and in which grade. Coins with low populations are, obviously, much more desirable than coins with high populations.

These are just some of the ways in which to collect Type Two Double Eagles. Part of the appeal of coin collecting is the myriad possibilities it offers the collector with imagination.

Type Two Double Eagles: Mintage Figures

1866	698,745	+ 30 Proofs
1866-S	842,250	
1867	251,015	+ 50 Proofs
1867-S	920,750	
1868	98,575	+ 25 Proofs
1868-S	837,500	
1869	175,130	+ 25 Proofs
1869-S	686,750	
1870	155,150	+ 35 Proofs
1870-CC	3,789	
1870-S	982,000	
1871	80,120	+ 30 Proofs
1871-CC	17,387	
1871-S	928,000	
1872	251,850	+ 30 Proofs
1872-CC	26,900	
1872-S	780,000	
1873 Closed 3 and Open 3	1,709,800	+ 25 Proofs (Closed 3 only)
1873-CC	22,410	
1873-S Closed 3 and Open 3	1,040,600	
1874	366,780	+ 20 Proofs
1874-CC	115,085	
1874-S	1,214,000	
1875	295,720	+ 20 Proofs
1875-CC	111,151	
1875-S	1,230,000	
1876	583,860	+ 45 Proofs
1876-CC	138,441	
1876-S	1,597,000	

By: Mike Fuljenz

1866

MINTAGE: 698,775
RARITY RANKING:
    Overall: 12th of 31   **By Mint:** 7th of 12
    Premium Quality: 13th of 31   **By Mint:** 6th of 12

    The 1866 Double Eagle is an extremely popular issue with collectors. Its popularity encompasses a broad range of interests and collecting habits. Some of the major reasons for this issue's popularity include the following:

- It is very popular with Civil War collectors who, after they complete their sets, typically move on to the post-Civil War issues.

- It is the first Double Eagle upon which the motto IN GOD WE TRUST appears.

- It is a first year of issue and it is the only Philadelphia Double Eagle dated 1866 (no coins were struck lacking the motto on the reverse.)

    This date tends to be found with a fairly good quality of strike. On the obverse, the hair of Liberty often shows weakness (as do the great majority of Type Two Double Eagles, regardless of date or mint) while the stars and border are mostly sharp. The reverse is usually very well struck. The surfaces frequently display very heavy bag abrasions and this is a very hard coin to find with a nominal amount of marks. The luster is mostly often a slightly grainy texture which is somewhat frosty. Specimens with reflective surfaces exist but these are quite hard to locate. Original, uncleaned pieces show coloration which ranges from medium orange-gold to a subdued rose-green hue and these often command premiums.

Most 1866 Double Eagles are unattractive due to excessive marks. It is not uncommon to find pieces which show significant Mint-made problems such as long, unattractive black carbon streaks. Other coins show insignificant problems such as copper spotting which is the result of an improper mixture of copper within the gold used to strike these pieces.

All business strikes of this date have a normal date. No major die varieties are known although it is very likely that a number of different date positions exist.

Proof 1866 Double Eagles are extremely rare. Of the 30 pieces originally struck, it is doubtful if more than 10-12 exist. The quality of these survivors is a bit choicer than one would expect and a few very nice Proofs exist. All examples show a spectacularly mispunched date with the first 1 originally punched down on the rim.

This date is fairly easy to locate in Extremely Fine and average quality About Uncirculated pieces exist in significant quantities. The 1866 Double Eagle becomes very scarce in the higher About Uncirculated grades and clean, original AU-53 to AU-58 coins are rare. In Mint State, the 1866 Double Eagle is a very rare coin.

RARITY:
Total Known: 650-750
Overall Rarity By Grade:

VF	EF	AU	MINT STATE
70-80	190-225	350-400	40-45

PRICE LEVELS:

AU-50:	$2,400 - 3,000
MS-60:	$11,000 - 13,000

CONDITION CENSUS:

In order to qualify for the Condition Census for this issue, a coin must grade at least Mint State-60.

NOTES

1866-S With Motto

MINTAGE: 842,250
RARITY RANKINGS:
    Overall: 14th of 31   **By Mint:** 3rd of 12
    Premium Quality: 12th of 31   **By Mint:** 3rd of 12

During the first two months of the year, 1866-S Double Eagles were struck with the old No Motto (i.e., Type One) reverse. Beginning in March, 1866, nearly three quarter of a million 1866-S Double Eagles were struck using the new With Motto (i.e., Type Two) reverse. Since there are two distinct issues, the 1866-S Double Eagle is known as a Transitional Issue. Such coins are extremely popular with collectors.

The 1866-S With Motto Double Eagle typically displays a rather soft strike. On the obverse, the hair below Liberty's tiara and on her bun is nearly always somewhat flat as is the area above her eye. The stars tend to be sharper and examples with full radial lines with the stars are not uncommon. The reverse will often show weakness on the shield and at the innermost parts of the wings. The borders are typically weak with the reverse rim showing a pronounced bevelled appearance. This is a product of the striking process and it does not affect the value of any coin which shows this phenomenon. The surfaces on most examples are very heavily abraded with deep marks in the fields and on the devices. The luster is often below average and it shows a peculiar granular frosty texture which is unique to this issue. Original, uncleaned pieces will display rich orange-gold and rose hues and these typically command strong premiums.

All genuine 1866-S With Motto Double Eagles have a tiny mintmark which is positioned atop the right serif of the N in TWENTY. Many pieces have a network of fine die cracks which join the lettering on the reverse. These are mint-made and they do not detract from the value of a coin.

While some very appealing 1866-S With Motto Double Eagles are known, many of the specimens offered to collectors have poor eye appeal. Very attractive pieces are very hard to find, regardless of their grade, and they typically command a hefty premium.

This date is scarce in all grades. It is usually found in Very Fine to Extremely Fine grades. About Uncirculated 1866-S Double Eagles almost always qualify at the lower end of this grade range. It becomes rare in AU-53, very rare in AU-58 and extremely rare in full Mint State.

RARITY:
Total Known: 850-1000
Overall Rarity By Grade:

VF	EF	AU	MINT STATE
125-150	425-500	294-343	9-10

PRICE LEVELS:

AU-50:	$4,000 - 5,000
MS-60:	$24,000 - 30,000

CONDITION CENSUS

To qualify for the Condition Census, an 1866-S With Motto Double Eagle must grade AU-58 or better. Premium quality About Uncirculated-55 specimens may also lay strong claim to qualification within the Condition Census for this issue.

1867

MINTAGE: 251,065
RARITY RANKING:
    Overall: 11th of 31   **By Mint:** 6th of 12
    Premium Quality: 15th of 31   **By Mint:** 7th of 12

The 1867 is the commonest Type Two Double Eagle struck at the Philadelphia Mint during the 1860's. In Uncirculated grades, it is easily the most plentiful date from this decade. Its availability in higher grades makes it very popular with beginning collectors who wish to own a very nice coin from this decade at an affordable price level.

1867 Double Eagles are among the best struck Type Two Double Eagles of any date. Most examples show very sharp strikes with just a bit of weakness on the hair of Liberty. The surfaces are almost always very extensively abraded with deep marks concentrated at the center of the obverse and in the fields. It is not unusual for examples of this date to have mint-made faults such as coppery spots or long black streaks in the planchet. The luster on most 1867 Double Eagles is excellent with a rich, very frosty texture. The typical coloration ranges from bright rose to green-gold and orange. It is possible to find a very attractive example of this date, although most of the coins with really good luster and color will show excessive marks. Coins with minimal marks command strong premiums.

No significant die varieties are known to exist.

While a total of 50 Proof 1867 Double Eagles were struck, it is very possible that as many as half of these were melted or went unsold. Today, this is an extremely rare date as a Proof with an estimated population of 9-11 coins.

The 1867 Double Eagle is almost never seen in lower grades. The typical survivor grades About Uncirculated-50 or a bit better and is characterized by heavily abraded surfaces. A sizable hoard of nice quality coins were discovered in Europe in the mid-1960's. These coins have no real wear but are frequently so heavily marked that the grading services net grade them down to the AU-55 or AU-58 level. Mint State 1867 Double Eagles can be obtained but finding a pleasing piece may take considerable effort. Most of these pieces grade MS-60 to MS-61. Any 1867 Double Eagle grading MS-62 or above is very rare.

RARITY:
Total Known: 550-650+
Overall Rarity By Grade:

VF	EF	AU	MINT STATE
25-30	75-95	250-300	200-225

PRICE LEVELS:

AU-50:	$1,400 - 1,800
MS-60:	$4,500 - 6,000

CONDITION CENSUS:

To qualify as a Condition Census example, an 1867 Double Eagle must grade Mint State-62 or better.

NOTES

1867-S

MINTAGE: 920,750
RARITY RANKING:
    Overall: 13th of 31   **By Mint:** 2nd of 12
    Premium Quality: 11th of 31   **By Mint:** 2nd of 12

    Despite its high mintage of nearly a million coins, the 1867-S Double Eagle is a scarce and very underrated date. It is the second rarest San Francisco Type Two Double Eagle in Mint State and the third rarest Type Two issue in terms of its overall rarity.

    This is one of the most difficult Type Two Double Eagles to find with a good strike. Virtually all known examples are quite flat on the hair of Liberty. In addition, many of the stars on the obverse are flat and do not show their full radial lines. The date sometimes is flat with the 6 and the 7 more weakly impressed than the 1 and the 8. The reverse is better struck. The center is mostly sharp with occasional areas of flatness seen at the shield and inner wings. Many 1867-S Double Eagles are heavily marked but the surfaces are generally cleaner than on Philadelphia Double Eagles from this year. For some reason, many coins have been cleaned and show heavy hairlines or scratches; these examples are excluded from encapsulation by both PCGS and NGC. The luster is typically subdued with a moderately frosty texture. The coloration on 1867-S Double Eagles ranges from deep green-gold to orange and coppery hues. Choice, original examples command significant premiums.

This is one of the most difficult Type Two Double Eagles to find with good eye appeal. The mediocre strike, heavy bagmarks and subdued luster seen on most pieces do not make for very attractive coins. Any very choice higher grade example should be purchased by the serious collector as it may take many months to locate another.

The mintmark on 1867-S is tiny and it is located over the right serif of the N in TWENTY.

1867-S Double Eagles are scarce in all grades. The typical specimen grades Extremely Fine. About Uncirculated-50 coins are about the best quality which the collector can locate. In the higher AU grades, this is a rare coin and it is extremely rare in full Mint State.

RARITY:
Total Known: 725-850
Overall Rarity By Grade:

VF	EF	AU	MINT STATE
100-125	350-375	269-342	14-18

PRICE LEVELS:

AU-50:	$1,900 - 2,300
MS-60:	$18,000 - 21,000

CONDITION CENSUS:

If an 1867-S Double Eagle grades AU-58 and it is choice for the grade, it qualifies as a Condition Census piece.

NOTES

1868

MINTAGE: 98,600
RARITY RANKING:
 Overall: 3rd of 31   **By Mint:** 1st of 12
 Premium Quality: 3rd of 31   **By Mint:** 1st of 12

The 1868 is the rarest Philadelphia Type Two Double Eagle. It is one of just two Philadelphia Type Two Double Eagles with an original mintage figure of fewer than 100,000 business strikes (the other is the 1871) and it presents the specialist in this series with a real challenge.

This is among the better produced Philadelphia issues of this type. The strike is generally quite sharp with very good detail noted on the hair of Liberty and on the obverse stars. The reverse is typically bold as well with strong feathers and wing tips on the eagle. Type Two Double Eagles are nearly always found with heavy abrasions and the 1868 is no exception. However, it is possible to find examples with fewer severe marks than on other dates from this era. The luster seen on 1868 Double Eagles is generally well above average. Many coins show very intense frosty luster and some semi-Prooflike to nearly fully Prooflike pieces are known. The coloration on original, uncleaned pieces is most often orange-gold or rose-green gold.

An interesting diagnostic feature exists on certain business strike and Proof 1868 Double Eagles. On the reverse, some denticles (or border beads) can be seen to the left and the right of the eagle's tail towards the scroll. These are clashmarks from the obverse and are mint-made. They do not negatively affect a coin's value.

A total of 25 Proof 1868 Double Eagles were struck. Approximately 10 of these are known today. An abnormally high number of Proofs have been certified by the two major grading services but this almost certainly represents numerous appearances of the same few coins.

Most 1868 Double Eagles grade Extremely Fine. This is a very scarce date in About Uncirculated and the great majority of survivors in this grade range are no better than AU-50. The 1868 Double Eagle is very rare in AU-55 and AU-58 and it is extremely rare in Mint State.

RARITY:
Total Known: 275-325
Overall Rarity:
By Grade:

VF	EF	AU	MINT STATE
48-60	100-120	120-136	7-9

PRICE LEVELS:

AU-50:	$3,500 - 4,500
MS-60:	$24,000 - 30,000

CONDITION CENSUS:

A coin grading AU-58 qualifies as Condition Census for this issue.

NOTES

1868-S

MINTAGE: 837,500
RARITY RANKING:
Overall: 20th of 31   **By Mint:**   7th of 12
Premium Quality: 16th of 31   **By Mint:**   5th of 12

The 1868-S Double Eagle is a coin which receives very little attention, even from specialists in the Type Two series. While plentiful in lower grades, this is a rare and very overlooked coin in higher grades.

As with the other San Francisco Double Eagles from this era, the 1868-S is typically found with a soft strike. The hair on the obverse rarely shows much in the way of fine detail and this pattern of strike is sometimes mistaken for wear. The obverse border will often show weakness on the radial lines of the stars and on the rim. The reverse is sharper but it is not uncommon for the wing tips and the lower portion of the right wing to not be fully struck up. Many 1868-S Double Eagles are heavily abraded and this is another date which is very hard to find with clean, unmarked surfaces. The luster is dull and somewhat grainy with a subdued semi- frosty texture. A few examples exist with very good luster and these are scarce, desirable coins which command a strong premium. The coloration is typical of other San Francisco coins of this era with deep rose-gold and orange-green hues seen on uncleaned, original pieces.

No significant die varieties are known. The mintmark is very small and squat. It is positioned over the right serif of the N in TWENTY.

The 1868-S Double Eagle is a fairly common coin in lower grades. The typical example is an unattractive, heavily marked Very Fine to Extremely Fine. The majority of the About Uncirculated 1868-S Double Eagles are AU-50 coins which, once again, have liberal marks and little eye appeal. This date becomes very scarce in AU-53 and it is rare in AU-58. In Mint State, the 1868-S is very rare.

RARITY:
Total Known: 1100-1200+
Overall Rarity By Grade:

VF	EF	AU	MINT STATE
70-80	600-625	450-500	18-20

PRICE LEVELS:

AU-50:	$1,900 - 2,300
MS-60:	$14,000 - 17,000

CONDITION CENSUS:

The grade level at which an 1868-S Double Eagle qualifies as Condition Census is Mint State-60. However, a very clean and sharply struck AU-58 coin would also receive serious consideration as a Condition Census example.

1869

MINTAGE: 175,155
RARITY RANKING:
Overall: 10th of 31   **By Mint:** 5th of 12
Premium Quality: 10th of 31   **By Mint:** 5th of 12

The 1869 is the second rarest Type Two Double Eagle struck at the Philadelphia Mint during the 1860's.

This is a well struck issue. It is possible that the reason for this has to do with William Barber replacing James Longacre as Chief Mint Engraver in 1869. Barber was, in general, more competent as an engraver than his predecessor and he may have decided to perform some minor changes on the Double Eagle. Many 1869 Double Eagles show good hair definition and sharply defined stars on the obverse. The reverse is usually also well struck. The surfaces on 1869 Double Eagles are often abraded although not as noticeably so as on the 1867 and 1868 Philadelphia issues. The luster is generally frosty and slightly subdued. Original, uncleaned pieces have bright green-gold or attractive rose and orange coloration. These command strong premiums among collectors and dealers. A number of pieces have been cleaned and it is not uncommon to find examples with varying degrees of mint-made planchet faults. All in all, this is a date which can be found with above average eye appeal.

There are no significant die varieties known to exist.

Only 25 Proofs were struck and it is estimated that between 10 and 12 pieces have survived. One of these is a spectacular Proof-66 coin which is reported to have traded in excess of $250,000 during the late 1980's bull market. It is one of the two finest Proof Type Two Double Eagles of any date which is known to exist.

The 1869 Double Eagle is most often found in Extremely Fine grades. It is moderately scarce in the lower About Uncirculated grades and it becomes quite rare in the higher About Uncirculated grades (AU-55 and above). Mint State coins are very rare, although they are definitely more available than the 1868. A few nice Uncirculated coins exist as well as a gorgeous Gem (graded MS-65 by PCGS) which was once included in the famous Norman Stack type set of United States coins.

RARITY:
Total Known: 450-500
Overall Rarity By Grade:

VF	EF	AU	MINT STATE
35-40	125-150	250-270	30-35

PRICE LEVELS:

AU-50:	$2,400 - 3,000
MS-60:	$9,000 - 12,000

CONDITION CENSUS:

The qualifying level for the Condition Census for 1869 Double Eagles is Mint State-60.

NOTES

1869-S

MINTAGE: 686,750
RARITY RANKING:

Overall: 22nd of 31	**By Mint:** 8th of 12
Premium Quality: 21st of 31	**By Mint:** 8th of 12

If a collector wishes to obtain a single San Francisco Type Two Double Eagle produced during the 1860's, the 1869-S is probably the date he will purchase. The relative availability of this coin (at least in lower grades) makes it a very popular type issue.

The quality of strike seen on 1869-S Double Eagles is not very good. The obverse shows an unusual somewhat concave appearance. This results in flat areas on the hair of Liberty as well as on the stars. Many of the stars show extra outlines where an engraver attempted to strengthen them. As this work was done inside the mint, it is considered a diagnostic characteristic and it does not affect a coin's value. As on so many of the San Francisco Double Eagles produced during this era, the surfaces on the typical 1869-S are liberally abraded. The luster is subdued and slightly grainy with a deep, frosty texture. Uncleaned pieces will show a range of colors which include rose-green, deeper green-gold and orange-gold hues. The level of eye appeal seen on most examples of this date is not very high. Coins which are attractive or which show a good strike are quite scarce and they carry strong premiums.

Two die varieties are known to exist. The more common has a normal reverse die. The rarer of the two has doubling on the reverse which can be seen most clearly at STATES OF and on the seven upper stars.

The 1869-S Double Eagle is plentiful in Very Fine and Extremely Fine grades. It becomes scarcer in About Uncirculated-53 and rare in About Uncirculated-58. A small group of Mint State-60 pieces entered the market a few years ago and they were very quickly absorbed by collectors. A tiny handful of very choice Uncirculated coins are known and these are greatly prized by their current owners.

RARITY:
Total Known: 1250-1500+
Overall Rarity By Grade:

VF	EF	AU	MINT STATE
90-100	510-640	600-700	50-60

PRICE LEVELS:

AU-50:	$1,600 - 2,000
MS-60:	$11,000 - 14,000

CONDITION CENSUS:

To be in the Condition Census, an 1869-S Double Eagle must grade at least Mint State-60 and it must represent premium quality at this grade level. This includes a strong strike, good luster and cleaner surfaces than usual.

1870

MINTAGE: 155,185
RARITY RANKINGS:
   Overall: 4th of 31   **By Mint:** 2nd of 12
   Premium Quality: 5th of 31   **By Mint:** 2nd of 12

The 1870 is one of the rarest Type Two Double Eagles. It is a scarce coin in all grades and a very rare one in premium quality. However, it still commands only a small premium over other dates of this type which are far more available. Many seasoned numismatists believe that the 1870 Double Eagle is an exceedingly undervalued coin.

This date generally shows an acceptable strike. While Liberty's hair is not usually all that well defined, the stars and other border details are quite sharp. The reverse also is very well struck with no major areas of weakness. Many 1870 Double Eagles have significant bag abrasions on their surfaces but it is possible to locate some clean, wholesome examples. Such coins are rare and often command a very high premium over "typical" pieces. The luster on most 1870 Double Eagles is good with a thick, frosty texture found on uncleaned, minimal worn specimens. This is a date which can be located with above average eye appeal. The date collector should be advised that "high end" 1870 Double Eagles are quite popular.

No significant die varieties are known to exist.

35 Proofs were struck. Approximately nine or ten are believed to have survived. Needless to say, these are extremely rare and highly desirable coins which generally only appear for sale at very important "name" auctions.

1870 Double Eagles are most often seen in Very Fine to Extremely Fine grades. This date is quite scarce in AU-50 and it becomes rare in AU-53 and higher grades. Mint State pieces are extremely rare.

RARITY:
Total Known: 280-340+
Overall Rarity By Grade:

VF	EF	AU	MINT STATE
45-55	105-125	120-150	12-15

PRICE LEVELS:

AU-50:	$4,000 - 5,000
MS-60:	$14,000 - 16,000

CONDITION CENSUS:

An 1870 Double Eagle which grades Choice About Uncirculated-58 qualifies as a Condition Census example.

NOTES

1870-CC

MINTAGE: 3,789
RARITY RANKINGS:
  Overall: 1st of 31   **By Mint:** 1st of 7
  Premium Quality: 1st of 31   **By Mint:** 1st of 7

The 1870-CC Double Eagle holds a number of important distinctions. It is the rarest and most valuable Type Two Double Eagle. It is the most famous and desirable gold coin struck at the Carson City Mint. And, it is the most difficult Type Two Double Eagle to locate in premium quality grades.

The quality of strike for this issue is not very good. The obverse always shows a weaker impression than on the reverse. The stars, especially those at the left, are blunt while Liberty's hair is flatly detailed. On the reverse, the wing feathers tend to show good detail while the borders are weaker. The tail feathers are always weak, as are the stars which encircle the motto. Every known 1870-CC Double Eagle is very heavily abraded. The fields nearly always show deep, detracting gouges while many pieces have conspicuous bumps on the rim from mishandling. This is an issue which obviously went directly into circulation and stayed there for some time. The luster on those few relatively high grade coins which exist is somewhat reflective. The coloration tends to be a medium orange-gold shade. Many survivors have been cleaned and the concept of "eye appeal" is alien when it comes to this date.

The reason for the uneven pattern of wear seen on this issue seems to be the result of technical difficulties at the Carson City Mint. When the coins were struck, they were not properly centered within the collar. As a result, the left obverse rim and the corresponding area on the reverse are narrower and more weakly impressed than on the right side of the coin. This characteristic is found on all examples of this date and it is a good test for the authenticity of any 1870-CC Double Eagle.

Two die varieties are known. On the first, the mintmark is located over the NT in TWENTY. On the second, the mintmark is placed over the upright stroke of the N in TWENTY.

The sales records of 1870-CC Double Eagles are as distinctive as their strike and appearance. Generally, this date becomes available in spurts. Two or three pieces will come onto the market, eventually be absorbed, and then disappear for many years. Then, it becomes nearly impossible to find a piece for sale. Nearly every example of this date is owned by a serious collector and these coins trade far less frequently than pieces owned by investors or dealers.

The 1870-CC Double Eagle is usually seen in bagmarked Very Fine grades. It is infrequently available in Extremely Fine and most of the few known EF's are no better than low-end EF-40 coins. Choice Extremely Fine pieces are exceedingly rare and there is no known 1870-CC Double Eagle which grades Mint State.

RARITY:
Total Known: 50-60+
Overall Rarity: High R-5

VF	EF	AU	MINT STATE
26-35	20-24	5	0

PRICE LEVELS:

EF-40:	$175,000 - 225,000
EF-45:	$250,000 - 300,000
AU-50:	$400,000 - 500,000

CONDITION CENSUS:

An 1870-CC Double Eagle grading Choice Extremely Fine qualifies as a Condition Census example.

NOTES

1870-S

MINTAGE: 982,000
RARITY RANKINGS:
    Overall: 15th of 31   **By Mint:** 4th of 12
    Premium Quality: 14th of 31   **By Mint:** 4th of 12

Despite its high mintage figure of nearly a million coins, the 1870-S is the second rarest Type Two Double Eagle in terms of its overall rarity and the fourth rarest in premium quality grades.

The 1870-S Double Eagle is nearly always found with a soft, somewhat "mushy" strike. This is especially true on the obverse. Liberty's hair shows poor definition on the curls and the stars seldom show their radial lines. On the reverse, the detail at the center is seldom full. Many 1870-S Double Eagles have their poor strikes compounded by the fact that they show heavily bagmarked surfaces. The luster tends to be a mixture of satiny bloom and Mint frost. Original, uncleaned pieces may show rose-gold or orange coloration. Locating an example of this date with good eye appeal is very difficult. The collector should be prepared to pay a strong premium for any coin which is well struck and which has relatively few marks.

There are no significant die varieties known. The mintmark is tiny and placed fairly low in the field over the middle of the right serif of the N in TWENTY.

Most 1870-S Double Eagles grade Very Fine to Extremely Fine. This date becomes scarce in About Uncirculated-53 and it is very scarce in About Uncirculated- 58. Mint State 1870-S Double Eagles are quite rare.

RARITY:
Total Known: 900-1100
Overall Rarity By Grade:

VF	EF	AU	MINT STATE
125-200	300-400	400-450	25-35

PRICE LEVELS:

AU-50:	$1,600 - 2,000
MS-60:	$7,500 - 10,000

CONDITION CENSUS:

An 1870-S Double Eagle which grades Mint State-60 and which is choice for the grade qualifies as a Condition Census example of this date.

NOTES

1871

MINTAGE: 80,150
RARITY RANKINGS:
  Overall: 7th of 31   **By Mint:** 4th of 12
  Premium Quality: 6th of 31   **By Mint:** 3rd of 12

The 1871 has the lowest mintage figure of any Philadelphia Type Two Double Eagle. It is one of the rarest coins of this type and its low mintage figure has always made it a very popular issue with collectors and investors.

This is one of the best produced Type Two Double Eagles. The quality of strike found on most pieces is far above average for this design. Liberty's hair may show some weakness but it is still far sharper than what is typically seen on the Type Two San Francisco and Carson City issues. Many 1871 Double Eagles show moderate to heavy bagmarks in the fields. It is possible to find a piece with clean surfaces and these coins command premiums with collectors. The luster on 1871 Double Eagles is very good. Higher grade specimens show intense frosty luster with a somewhat satiny texture. A few semi-Prooflike pieces exist; these are generally rather heavily bagmarked. Original, uncleaned 1871 Double Eagles tend to display rose-gold and pale green coloration.

Two die varieties exist. On the first, the 71 in the date almost touch and the serifs on the 1's in the date are long. On the second, the 71 are further apart and the serifs on the 1's in the date are shorter.

30 Proofs were struck. Approximately eight or nine of these exist. As with all Proof Type Two Double Eagles, this is an exceedingly rare issue which is almost never offered for sale.

The 1871 Double Eagle is a scarce coin in all grades. When available, the typical specimen will grade in the Extremely Fine-40 to Extremely Fine-45 range. In About Uncirculated-53, the 1871 Double Eagle becomes very scarce and it is legitimately rare in the higher AU grades. Mint State pieces are rare but a small number of very choice (Mint State-63 to Mint State-64) pieces exist. It is possible that a tiny hoard of these entered the market sometime in the 1980's as these coins tend to have a similar overall appearance. We are aware of at least one MS-63 1871 Double Eagle trading in excess of $30,000 in 1989; none appear to have been offered for sale in the past few years.

RARITY:
Total Known: 375-450+
Overall Rarity By Grade:

VF	EF	AU	MINT STATE
50-60	115-150	175-200	30-35

PRICE LEVELS:

AU-50: $3,500 - 4,000
MS-60: $10,000 - 12,000

CONDITION CENSUS:

An 1871 Double Eagle which grades Mint State-60 and which is choice for the grade qualifies as a Condition Census example of this date.

NOTES

1871-CC

MINTAGE: 17,387
RARITY RANKINGS:
  Overall: 2nd of 31   **By Mint:** 2nd of 7
  Premium Quality: 2nd of 31   **By Mint:** 2nd of 7

    The 1871-CC is the most difficult Type Two Double Eagle for the collector of average means to acquire. It is a rare coin in all grades and it is extremely hard to find in premium quality grades.

    This date comes with a better overall quality of strike than the 1870-CC Double Eagle. The detail on Liberty's hair is much more full than on the 1870-CC, although it is still somewhat weak in comparison to a Philadelphia issue of this design. Most 1871-CC Double Eagles are strongly detailed at the borders and many show full radial lines within the stars. The reverse is also sharp. The luster on most pieces is satiny with a slight amount of Prooflike reflectiveness. It should be pointed out, though, that most 1871-CC Double Eagles are worn enough that they show little—or no— luster. The surfaces on most 1871-CC Double Eagles are very heavily abraded. The coloration is most often a rich green-gold and uncleaned higher grade pieces may have rich coppery-gold overtone. "High end" pieces are very rare and they command a significant premium over typical quality pieces.

No significant die varieties are known. The mintmark is placed fairly far to the left with the second about halfway over the serif of the N in TWENTY. The first C is higher than the second C.

The 1871-CC Double Eagle is most often seen in Very Fine grades. It is sometimes available in Extremely Fine with the typical EF example showing liberal marks and poor eye appeal. In About Uncirculated, the 1871-CC is a rare coin and nearly every known example in this grade range is no better than an AU-50. In AU-53 to AU-58, this issue is extremely rare and it is doubtful if more than two or three Mint State coins exist.

RARITY:
Total Known: 250-275+
Overall Rarity By Grade:

VF	EF	AU	MINT STATE
80-85	100-107	75-85	2-3

PRICE LEVELS:

AU-50:	$50,000 - 60,000
MS-60:	$120,000 - 150,000

CONDITION CENSUS:

An 1871-CC Double Eagle which grades About Uncirculated-55 will definitely qualify as a Condition Census example of this date. A coin grading AU-53 which is choice for the grade might also qualify.

1871-S

MINTAGE: 928,000
RARITY RANKINGS:
    Overall: 19th of 31   **By Mint:** 6th of 12
    Premium Quality: 19th of 31   **By Mint:** 6th of 12

    The 1871-S is one of the scarcer Type Two Double Eagles struck at the San Francisco Mint in terms of the total number known to exist. Interestingly, it is one of the easier issues of this type from this mint to locate in higher grades.

    The quality of strike for the 1871-S Double Eagle is somewhat irregular. For the most part, this is a well struck issue but many pieces show curiously weak stars on the left obverse in contrast to sharp stars at the right or vice versa. On coins where the stars are irregularly impressed, the border at one side tends to be thinner than at the other. It should be stressed that this is a mint-caused phenomenon and it does not affect the coin's value. The surfaces on most 1871-S Double Eagles show liberal abrasions as these coins tended to be roughly transported in bags. This is an issue which has very good luster. It ranges from extremely frosty to a satiny, slightly granular texture. The coloration on uncleaned 1871-S Double Eagles can vary from rich rose-gold to a deeper greenish coloration. This date can be found with above average eye appeal and very pleasing coins make good San Francisco type coins.

No major die varieties are known. The mintmark is very small and low; it is positioned over the right serif of the N in TWENTY.

1871-S Double Eagles are most often seen in Extremely Fine grades. This date is moderately scarce in About Uncirculated-50 and it is hard to locate in AU-53 and higher grades. Mint State pieces are rare but have become a bit more available in recent years due to a very small hoard which has recently entered the market. Most experts recognize this date as the first Type Two Double Eagle (with the exception of the 1867) which is still sometimes located in small group in overseas sources. If a collector is worried about buying dates which have the potential for more hoards existing, he should concentrate on the coins dated prior to 1871.

Almost every known Uncirculated 1871-S Double Eagle grades Mint State-60. Higher graded coins are very scarce.

RARITY:
Total Known: 1050-1150+
Overall Rarity By Grade:

VF	EF	AU	MINT STATE
70-100	325-350	550-600	100-115

PRICE LEVELS:

AU-50:	$1,600 - 2,000
MS-60:	$6,000 - 7,500
MS-63:	$30,000 - 35,000

CONDITION CENSUS:

To qualify for the Condition Census, an 1871-S Double Eagle must grade Mint State-61. A coin grading MS-60 could be considered Condition Census if it displayed above-average surfaces and luster and it were well struck.

NOTES

1872

MINTAGE: 251,880
RARITY RANKINGS:
   Overall: 16th of 31   **By Mint:** 9th of 12
   Premium Quality: 17th of 31   **By Mint**: 8th of 12

   The 1872 Double Eagle has a mintage figure which is virtually identical to the 1867. The 1872 is a rarer coin in terms of the total number known to exist. It is scarcer than the 1867 in Mint State but it can be located in higher grades more easily than the 1868-1870 Philadelphia Double Eagles.

   This issue is most often seen with a good quality of strike. It is possible to locate a specimen with well-defined hair, sharp stars and a crisply detailed reverse. It is not as easy, however, to find a piece which has clean surfaces. Many 1872 Double Eagles are very heavily abraded and examples with reasonably mark-free surfaces command a premium. The luster on this issue is usually good. Some pieces are Prooflike while others are very frosty. The frosty coins are generally considered preferable as these do not show bagmarks as prominently as their reflective Prooflike counterparts. Uncleaned, original 1872 Double Eagles have coloration which ranges from orange-gold to rose and green-gold. Pieces with good eye appeal as a result of minimal marks, good color and no signs of cleaning generally command a premium over typical quality examples.

No significant die varieties exist.

30 Proof 1872 Double Eagles were produced. It is believed that ten or so exist. The finest of these is a spectacular Proof-66 which was part of an original 1872 gold proof set sold as part of the James Stack collection in March, 1995.

The 1872 Double Eagle can be located in Extremely Fine and About Uncirculated grades without a great degree of difficulty. Many of the examples which grade About Uncirculated-53 to About Uncirculated-58 are unappealing and "high end" specimens are harder to obtain than one might anticipate. This date can sometimes be located in Mint State-60. It is very scarce in MS-61 and very rare in any grade higher than this.

RARITY:
Total Known: 850-1000
Overall Rarity By Grade:

VF	EF	AU	MINT STATE
50-60	200-270	500-550	100-120

PRICE LEVELS:

AU-50:	$1,400 - 1,600
MS-60:	$6,000 - 7,500
MS-63:	$45,000 - 55,000

CONDITION CENSUS:

An 1872 Double Eagle grading Mint State-61 qualifies as Condition Census. A very high end MS-60 coin with cleaner than usual surfaces, nice luster and good color may qualify as well.

NOTES

1872-CC

MINTAGE: 26,900
RARITY RANKINGS:
   Overall: 5th of 31   **By Mint:** 3rd of 7
   Premium Quality: 4th of 31   **By Mint:** 3rd of 7

    The 1872-CC is a very popular date. While rare in higher grades, this is the earliest issue Double Eagle from the fabled Carson City Mint which can be easily obtained by the collector of average means. This is a date which evokes rich historic connotations as, in 1872, the "Wild West" was still truly a wild place.

    The quality of strike seen on 1872-CC Double Eagles is surprisingly good. This is quite unusual as nearly every other gold coin struck at the Carson City Mint in 1872 (half eagles and eagles were also produced) was very poorly manufactured. On the obverse, the stars are often completely detailed while the hair is sharp for a coin of this design. The reverse is also sharp although the stars surrounding the motto tend to be slightly flat. The luster is typically good with a soft, satiny texture seen on higher grade specimens. The surfaces on the typical 1872-CC Double Eagle show a number of abrasions but this date is more easily located with acceptable surfaces than the 1870-CC or the 1871-CC. There are some coins which exist with old test marks on their edges. These are a reminder of a scandal which rocked the Carson City Mint in 1873. It was learned that a number of lightweight, debased coins dated 1872-CC and 1873-CC were struck and these test marks reflect samples taken from suspected coins. As long as these marks are not too severe the major grading services will encapsulate them and they do not affect the value of a piece which displays them.

1872-CC Double Eagles with good eye appeal do exist although they can be hard to locate. A coin which has good luster, a sharp strike and clean surfaces generally commands a very strong premium over a typical quality example.

Two die varieties are known. On the first, the mintmark is closely spaced while on the second the mintmark is wider. It is not known which of these two is rarer.

This date is not rare in lower grades. It becomes scarce in nice Extremely Fine-45 and it is very scarce in About Uncirculated-53. It is a rare coin in AU-55 and higher grades and it is excessively rare in strict Mint State.

RARITY:
Total Known: 350-400+
Overall Rarity By Grade:

VF	EF	AU	MINT STATE
35-50	180-190	133-157	2-3

PRICE LEVELS:

AU-50:	$14,000 - 17,000
MS-60:	$45,000 - 55,000
MS-63:	_____

CONDITION CENSUS:

An 1872-CC Double Eagle which grades Choice About Uncirculated-55 qualifies as a Condition Census example of this date.

NOTES

1872-S

MINTAGE: 780,000
RARITY RANKINGS:
   Overall: 18th of 31   **By Mint:** 5th of 12
   Premium Quality: 20th of 31   **By Mint:** 7th of 12

The 1872-S is one of the more obtainable Type Two Double Eagles struck at the San Francisco Mint.

This date is not as well struck as some of the other San Francisco Double Eagles from this era. On the obverse, the date is thin and appears weaker than usual. The stars at the top of the obverse are sometimes flat and it is rare for all of the stars to show their radial lines. Liberty's hair is flat as well. On the reverse, the strike is a bit sharper. The typical 1872-S Double Eagle has very heavily abraded surfaces. The luster is mostly frosty with a slightly subdued appearance. Uncleaned pieces will display pleasing rose-green or orange-gold coloration and such coins command a premium. This is a date which can prove hard to locate an example with good overall eye appeal. An 1872-S Double Eagle which has relatively clean surfaces, a sharper than usual strike and no signs of cleaning is hard to locate and such coins command a strong premium among collectors.

The mintmark is small and squat and it positioned centrally over the N in TWENTY. No significant die varieties are currently known.

The 1872-S Double Eagle is most often seen in Extremely Fine grades. It can be obtained in About Uncirculated-50 through About Uncirculated-53 grades without much difficulty. It becomes somewhat scarce in AU-55, very scarce in AU-58 and rare in Mint State. This date remains rare in any grade above MS-60.

RARITY:
Total Known: 975-1100+
Overall Rarity By Grade:

VF	EF	AU	MINT STATE
115-130	225-260	575-650	70-80

PRICE LEVELS:

AU-50:	$1,400 - 1,600
MS-60:	$4,500 - 5,500
MS-63:	$30,000 - 35,000

CONDITION CENSUS:

To qualify as a Condition Census coin, an 1872-S Double Eagle must grade Mint State-61.

NOTES

THE CLOSED 3 AND OPEN 3 VARIETIES OF 1873

CLOSED 3   **OPEN 3**

The Double Eagles of 1873 are marked by one of the most interesting varieties seen on any series of United States gold coins; the Closed 3 and Open 3.

One of the responsibilities of the Mint Engraver is to prepare date punches or logotypes. Generally speaking, the logotypes for a specific year are prepared at the end of the previous year. In November 1872, Mint Engraver William Barber created the date punches for what would be the working dies for the 1873 issues. On these punches, Barber produced the digit 3 in such a way that the knobs were much too close. As a result, this digit closely resembled the numeral 8.

In the Archives of the Mint, there exists a letter dated January 18, 1873 from Chief Coiner A.L. Snowden to Mint Director James Pollock which makes note of this and which lodges a formal complaint. As a result, Barber was ordered to make up new date punches which had a more distinctive number 3.

1873 Double Eagles were struck with both style of date punch. The Philadelphia coins were mostly struck with an Open 3. The Closed 3 coins from this mint are considerably scarcer and all of the 25 Proofs struck exhibit this date punch as well. The San Francisco coins were mostly struck employing the Closed 3 punch and the Open 3 coins from this mint are considerably harder to locate. All of the 1873 Double Eagles struck at the Carson City Mint have a Closed 3.

While certain collectors were aware of these varieties, they remained mostly unknown until the publication of Harry X. Boosel's "1873-1873" in 1960. In this book, Boosel listed all of the known varieties of 1873 coinage as well as important historical background. This book is out-of-print and somewhat difficult to find but it is an important addition to the library of any serious Type Two Double Eagle collector.

1873 CLOSED 3

MINTAGE: Unknown
RARITY RANKINGS:
    Overall: 6th of 31   **By Mint:** 3rd of 12
    Premium Quality: 8th of 31   **By Mint:** 4th of 12

    A total of 1,709,800 business strike 1873 Double Eagles were produced at the Philadelphia Mint. The great majority of these are of the Open 3 variety. The Closed 3 1873 Double Eagle is many times rarer than its Open 3 counterpart. Considering how many pieces exist and comparing this to other Type Two Philadelphia Double Eagles with a similar overall rarity, it is probable that around 100,000 pieces were struck.

    The quality of strike for the 1873 Closed 3 Double Eagle is not as good as that found on the 1873 Open 3. Many Closed 3 coins are not fully impressed on the hair of Liberty and show weakness on the stars as well. The reverse tends to be a bit sharper but it is rarely seen with complete definition at the centers. The surfaces are nearly always found with very heavy abrasions. Any example of this variety which does not show deep, dense nicks commands a strong premium over a "typical" example. The luster on most examples is good with a very frosty texture most often seen. The coloration on original, uncleaned pieces is often a green-gold hue with rose or orange-gold shadings. The level of eye appeal for this date is generally below average; mostly as a result of the aforementioned surface abrasions seen on most coins.

A total of 25 Proof 1873 Closed 3 Double Eagles were struck. Approximately eight to ten pieces exist and this issue is a great rarity. While one or two of these Proofs are very choice, a number have been cleaned and/or slightly mishandled.

The 1873 Closed 3 Double Eagle is most often seen in Extremely Fine and the lower end About Uncirculated grades. While scarce in all grades, this variety becomes legitimately rare in About Uncirculated-55 and it is very rare in Uncirculated. Most Uncirculated coins which are currently known show very heavy abrasions and grade no better than MS-60.

RARITY:
Total Known: 350-400+
Overall Rarity:
By Grade:

VF	EF	AU	MINT STATE
50-60	90-110	170-200	40-50

PRICE LEVELS:

AU-50:	$1,500 - 1,800
MS-60:	$3,600 - 4,200
MS-63:	————————

CONDITION CENSUS:

An 1873 Closed 3 Double Eagle which grades Mint State-60 qualifies for the Condition Census.

1873 OPEN 3

MINTAGE: 1,709,000 (less an unknown number of 1873 Closed 3 coins)
RARITY RANKINGS:
   Overall: 31st of 31   **By Mint:**   12th of 12
   Premium Quality: 31st of 31   **By Mint:**   12th of 12

The 1873 Open 3 is the most common Type Two Double Eagle. Because of this, it is a coin which is in great demand among type collectors who are seeking to add one nice Type Two Double Eagle to their collection.

This is an issue which can be found with a sharp strike. The typical example shows a sharper impression than the 1873 Closed 3 as well as most other Philadelphia Type Two Double Eagles. The surfaces are usually abraded but they tend to be cleaner than on 1873 Closed 3 Double Eagles. It is possible to locate examples with relatively few serious marks on the surfaces and these coins invariably command strong premiums due to their popularity as type pieces. The luster on many 1873 Open 3 Double Eagles is excellent with a thick, frosty texture. The coloration on uncleaned, original specimens can range from coppery-orange to reddish-gold to medium green-gold. Some coins show Mint-made copper spots on their surfaces. These spots do not detract from the value of a coin unless they are extremely pronounced.

A variety is known to exist which shows sharp doubling on the word LIBERTY. This variety is scarce and it commands a premium among collectors. The finest known example to me is an MS-63 which I assisted a collector with.

No Proof 1873 Open 3 Double Eagles were struck.

The 1873 Open 3 Double Eagle is very common in all circulated grades and it can be located in MS-60 and MS-61 grades without difficulty. MS-62 examples are moderately scarce but they can still be found at most large coin shows. In MS-63, this issue becomes very scarce and it is very rare in any grade higher than this. An extremely small number of MS-64 coins are known and these are extremely popular with collectors seeking very high grade type examples.

RARITY:
Total Known: 5800-7000+
Overall Rarity By Grade:

VF	EF	AU	MINT STATE
200-300	800-950	1800-2400	3000-3500

PRICE LEVELS:

AU-50:	$1,200 - 1,500
MS-60:	$1,800 - 2,200
MS-63:	$14,000-17,000

CONDITION CENSUS:

An 1873 Open 3 Double Eagle which grades Mint State-63 qualifies as a Condition Census example for this issue.

The 1873 Open 3 Double Eagle shows
strong doubling on the word LIBERTY.

1873-S CLOSED 3

MINTAGE: 1,040,600 (Less an unknown number of Open 3 coins)
RARITY RANKINGS:

Overall:	23rd of 31	**By Mint:**	9th of 12
Premium Quality:	23rd of 31	**By Mint:**	9th of 12

The 1873-S Closed 3 is easily the more common of the two varieties of Double Eagles struck at the San Francisco Mint in 1873. As recently as a few years ago, the 1873-S was a hard coin to find in all grades. However, a number of pieces have been located in European bank holdings.

1873-S Closed 3 Double Eagles are often weakly struck on the obverse. The hair above Liberty's hair and ear is almost always flat and the hair bun is weak as well. The stars at the left of the obverse are sometimes weaker than those on the right; this is the result of uneven pressure during the striking process and it does not adversely affect the value of a coin. The surfaces on most 1873-S Closed 3 Double Eagles are heavily abraded. This is due to the fact that many coins were shipped to foreign banks and were poorly handled. The luster is frosty with a slightly grainy texture. Uncleaned, original pieces typically display rose-gold and light green coloration. The level of eye appeal on most pieces is acceptable but it is very hard to locate pieces which are not heavily marked. 1873-S Closed 3 Double Eagles with relatively few severe marks are worth a strong premium.

No significant die varieties are known. The mintmark is very small and it positioned between the right edge of the N and the T in TWENTY.

The 1873-S Closed 3 has become an easy issue to locate in all circulated grades. In Uncirculated grades it is scarce, although pieces grading MS-60 and MS-61 can be obtained with some patience. This issue becomes very rare in MS-62 and is rarely seen in grades higher than this.

RARITY:
Total Known: 1300-1500+
Overall Rarity By Grade:

VF	EF	AU	MINT STATE
90-110	150-175	800-900	275-325

PRICE LEVELS:

AU-50:	$1,300 - 1,600
MS-60:	$2,800 - 3,500
MS-63:	$25,000 - 30,000

CONDITION CENSUS:

To qualify for the Condition Census, an 1873-S Closed 3 must grade at least MS-62.

NOTES

1873-S Open 3

MINTAGE: Unknown
RARITY RANKINGS:
    Overall: 8th of 31   **By Mint:**   1st of 12
    Premium Quality: 9th of 31   **By Mint:**   1st of 12

     The 1873-S Open 3 is easily the rarest of the two varieties of Double Eagle which were produced at the San Francisco Mint in 1873. This variety is, in fact, the rarest Type Two San Francisco Double Eagle in terms of its overall rarity.

     The quality of strike for this variety is somewhat similar to that seen on the 1873-S Closed 3. On the Open 3 coins, the obverse almost always shows incomplete details on the hair of Liberty. In addition, the left stars are often weaker than those on the right. The reverse will show some weakness at the center but it is sharper overall than the obverse. The surfaces on nearly every known example of this date show extremely heavy abrasions and the few relatively abrasion-free pieces which are available are highly prized by collectors. The luster on the typical 1873-S Open 3 Double Eagle is frosty with an underlying grainy texture. Coloration on original, uncleaned specimens is most often a rose-gold and orange hue with some specimens showing a greenish overtone. The level of eye appeal on most known 1873-S Open 3 Double Eagles is poor, primarily due to subpar strikes and extensive marks. An example which shows above-average eye appeal is very desirable and generally commands a strong premium among collectors.

No significant die varieties are known.

Until recently, the 1873-S Open 3 Double Eagle was a rare coin in any grade. As it has become better known, a number of specimens have been discovered by collectors. In addition, small groups of these have been located in overseas banks.

This variety is still scarce in all grades and it is most often seen in the lower About Uncirculated range. It becomes very scarce in AU-55 and better and it is still quite rare in Mint State. It appears that the 1873-S Open 3 is a true rarity in any grade higher than MS-60.

RARITY:
Total Known: 400-475+
Overall Rarity By Grade:

VF	EF	AU	MINT STATE
50-60	75-125	225-250	35-45

PRICE LEVELS:

AU-50:	$2,000 - 2,500
MS-60:	$12,000 - 15,000

CONDITION CENSUS:

An 1873-S Open 3 Double Eagle which grades MS-60 qualifies as Condition Census for this variety.

1873-CC

MINTAGE: 22,410
RARITY RANKINGS:
    Overall: 9th of 31   **By Mint:** 4th of 7
    Premium Quality: 7th of 31   **By Mint:** 4th of 7

    Until recently, the 1873-CC Double Eagle was considered to be a rarer coin than the 1872-CC. Due to a small hoard of coins which has entered the market between 1993 and the present, the 1873-CC is now a bit easier to locate than the 1872-CC. However, this is still a very rare coin in premium quality grades.

    The strike seen on most 1873-CC Double Eagles is sharp. While some of the stars on the obverse are not fully defined, most will be well detailed. The hair of Liberty shows the typical flatness seen on all Type Two Double Eagles while the reverse is generally quite sharp with the exception of the tips of the eagle's tail feathers and some of the stars around the motto. The luster is not as good as on the 1872-CC. It tends to have a somewhat "washed-out" satiny texture or it may be lightly Prooflike. The surfaces on most examples show very heavy abrasions. A few very clean pieces are known and these generally sell for a strong premium. The coloration can range from a bright yellow-gold hue to a deep green-gold shade. Pieces are sometimes seen with minor planchet imperfections or small black "grease stains." If these are unobtrusively positioned, they will not affect the value of a higher grade coin.

All 1873-CC Double Eagles have a Closed 3 in the date. The mintmark is very small with the second C over the right part of the serif of the N in TWENTY. No significant die varieties exist.

This date is most often seen in Very Fine and Extremely Fine grades. Lower quality About Uncirculated pieces are scarce but obtainable. The 1873-CC Double Eagle becomes very scarce in AU-55 and higher grades and it is a very rare coin in any Mint State grade.

RARITY:
Total Known: 450-550+
Overall Rarity By Grade:

VF	EF	AU	MINT STATE
71-116	175-200	200-225	14-18

PRICE LEVELS:

AU-50:	$15,000 - 16,000
MS-60:	$45,000 - 55,000

CONDITION CENSUS:

An 1873-CC Double Eagle which grades AU-58 qualifies as a Condition Census example of this date.

NOTES

1874

MINTAGE: 366,800
RARITY RANKINGS:
    Overall: 17th of 31   **By Mint:** 8th of 12
    Premium Quality: 18th of 31   **By Mint:** 9th of 12

While generally regarded as a very common date, the 1874 Double Eagle is actually scarcer than most collectors realize. This is the most difficult of the "late date" Philadelphia Type Two Double Eagles and it is harder to locate than some of the more highly regarded issues from the 1860's as well.

The quality of strike seen on this issue is often very bold. It is not uncommon to find examples with fully defined radial lines in the stars, sharp hair detail on the head of Liberty and bold wing tips. On some pieces, the denticles show some minor area of weakness, probably as a result of the die having deteriorated. 1874 Double Eagles are nearly always found with heavily marked surfaces. Most pieces show deep marks concentrated in the obverse fields and, to a lesser degree, on the reverse. The luster on the typical example is very good with a rich, frosty texture most often seen. Coloration on uncleaned 1874 Double Eagles ranges from bright green-gold to a paler rose and gold shade. Locating an 1874 Double Eagle with good eye appeal is difficult. Any example which shows minimal marks, good luster and no signs of having been cleaned is greatly prized by collectors and invariably trades for a strong premium.

This date is popular with collectors as it is the most feasible year in the Type Two era (1866-1876) to assemble a high grade complete denomination set ($1.00, $2.50, $3.00, $5.00, $10.00 and $20.00). An 1874 gold year set can be completed in Mint State with the exception of the $5.00 which is seldom seen above Extremely Fine.

No significant die varieties are known.

A total of 20 Proofs were struck. It is estimated that seven to nine of these exist today with the finest being a lovely NGC Proof-64 which is part of the Ed Trompeter Collection of United States proof gold coins.

The 1874 Double Eagle is usually found in the lower About Uncirculated grades. Due to the existence of a small group of coins located in Europe a few years ago, Mint State-60 pieces, while scarce, are sometimes available. This date becomes rare in Mint State-61, very rare in Mint State-62 and is extremely rare in any Uncirculated grade higher than this.

RARITY:
Total Known: 800-900+
Overall Rarity By Grade:

VF	EF	AU	MINT STATE
50-60	125-170	450-500	170-200

PRICE LEVELS:

AU-50:	$1,300 - 1,500
MS-60:	$2,500 - 3,500
MS-63:	$25,000 - 30,000

CONDITION CENSUS:

An 1874 Double Eagle which grades Mint State-62 is considered a Condition Census example.

NOTES

1874-CC

MINTAGE: 115,085
RARITY RANKINGS:
Overall: 26th of 31   **By Mint:** 5th of 7
Premium Quality: 22nd of 31   **By Mint:** 5th of 7

The 1874-CC has the second highest mintage figure of any Double Eagle struck at the Carson City Mint. It is a common coin in lower grades but it is scarce in higher grades.

The quality of strike seen on 1874-CC Double Eagles is comparable to that seen on the 1872-CC and 1873-CC Double Eagles. Liberty's hair is often flat, especially below the coronet and the ear. The stars are often blunt and show only a few radial lines. The reverse generally shows a better overall impression although many pieces are weak on the shield and along the outlines of the wings. Many coins show what appears to be serious weakness on the arrowheads. This is, in fact, a lapped die (caused by a Mint employee overzealously polishing the reverse die in attempt to remove a defect of some sort) and it does not affect the value of a coin. The surfaces on most 1874-CC Double Eagles are heavily abraded, as is common on nearly any Carson City Double Eagle regardless of date. The luster is most often semi-Prooflike with a satiny texture in the outlying portions of the fields. The coloration on original, uncleaned coins is bright yellow-gold or deeper green-gold. It is very hard to find an example of this date with good eye appeal. Any piece which is clean, lustrous and shows no signs of having been cleaned is considered very desirable. Such coins always trade for substantial premiums among collectors.

The mintmark is compact with the second C higher than the first. No significant die varieties are currently known but it is likely that at least a few exist.

The 1874-CC Double Eagle is relatively common in any grade up to and including About Uncirculated-50. It becomes scarce in the higher AU grades and rare in AU-58. A small hoard of pieces was well-distributed into the coin market in 1994 and this issue remains quite rare in the highest AU grades and full Mint State.

RARITY:
Total Known: 1750-2000+
Overall Rarity By Grade:

VF	EF	AU	MINT STATE
230-275	700-800	800-900	18-22

PRICE LEVELS:

AU-50:	$4,500 - 5,500
MS-60:	$15,000 - 18,000

CONDITION CENSUS:

An 1874-CC Double Eagle which grades Mint State-60 qualifies as a Condition Census example.

NOTES

1874-S

MINTAGE: 1,214,000
RARITY RANKINGS:
  Overall: 24th of 31   **By Mint:** 10th of 12
  Premium Quality: 25th of 31   **By Mint:** 10th of 12

The 1874-S Double Eagle is usually lumped together with the 1875-S and the 1876-S when measuring its degree of rarity. The 1874-S is, however, a substantially scarcer coin both in terms of its overall rarity and its premium quality rarity.

This is not an issue which can be easily located with a good quality of strike. The hair of Liberty is very poorly defined with little detail noted on the bun and the uppermost curls. The stars are often seen with poorly defined radial lines and they are sometimes much weaker on the right side of the obverse than on the left side. The reverse comes with a better strike but the shield is nearly always weak. Many 1874-S Double Eagles are very heavily abraded. The obverse fields may show very deep, clustered marks while the reverse is often heavily bagmarked as well. The luster on 1874-S Double Eagles ranges from very frosty to a slightly grainy satiny texture. Uncleaned specimens show coloration ranging from rose-green to orange- gold. This is yet another Type Two Double Eagle which is difficult to locate with good eye appeal. Pieces which are very attractive trade for strong premiums.

Two die varieties are known. On the first, the mintmark is very small and squat and it is positioned well to the right of the N in TWENTY. On the second, the mintmark is a bit taller, more to the left and clearly double punched with the first punch too low. The second variety appears to be considerably scarcer than the first.

The 1874-S Double Eagle is an underrated issue which is typically seen in Extremely Fine and low-end About Uncirculated grades. It is scarce in Mint State-60 and Mint State-61 and it becomes very rare in any grade higher than this. The finest piece of which we are aware is a very choice PCGS graded MS-63 in a well-known private collection.

RARITY:
Total Known: 1500-1750
Overall Rarity By Grade:

VF	EF	AU	MINT STATE
60-80	140-170	1100-1200	250-300

PRICE LEVELS:

AU-50:	$1,300 - 1,600
MS-60:	$2,400 - 3,000
MS-63:	$30,000 - 36,000

CONDITION CENSUS:

An 1874-S Double Eagle which grades MS-62 is considered a Condition Census example of this date.

NOTES

1875

MINTAGE: 295,740
RARITY RANKINGS:
   Overall: 21st of 31   **By Mint:** 10th of 12
   Premium Quality: 24th of 31   **By Mint:** 10th of 12

The 1875 is among the more common Philadelphia Type Two Double Eagles. Along with the 1873 Open 3 and the 1876, this date is very popular as a type coin. It is among the first issues which Type Two date collectors obtain as well.

This is typically a well struck coin. As with the majority of Type Two Double Eagles, the 1875 tends to show incomplete detail on the hair of Liberty. But the rest of the centers and the peripheries are found with sharp, clear details. Most 1875 Double Eagles are very heavily abraded. It is probable that many examples of this date never saw actual circulation. Instead, they were shipped from the Philadelphia Mint to various banks (in America and overseas) and in the process, they acquired a host of bagmarks. The luster on most 1875 Double Eagles is excellent with a rich, frosty texture most common. A few Prooflike coins are known and these are scarce. The coloration on 1875 Double Eagles ranges from rose-green to orange-gold. Many uncleaned higher grade examples show very nice coloration. It is possible to find an 1875 Double Eagle with good eye appeal although most examples are liberally marked.

A very interesting die variety exists for this date. A small number of pieces show what appear to be cancellation marks through the designer's initials (J.B.L.) which are located on the base of the neck of Liberty. It is not known exactly why these marks exist although it has been surmised that they may have been placed there out of spite or jealousy by another Mint employee. The "canceled obverse" 1875 Double Eagle is rare and it often sells for a substantial premium.

A total of 20 Proof 1875 Double Eagles were struck. This is the rarest and most highly prized Proof Type Two Double Eagle. Approximately six or seven pieces exist with at least three of these permanently impounded in museum collections.

The 1875 Double Eagle is generally found in the upper About Uncirculated grades. Mint State-60 pieces are fairly common while MS-61 and MS-62's can be obtained with a bit of patience. This date becomes rare in MS-63 and it is exceedingly rare in any grade higher than this.

RARITY:
Total Known: 1250-1500+
Overall Rarity By Grade:

VF	EF	AU	MINT STATE
50-60	100-140	400-500	700-800

PRICE LEVELS:

AU-50:	$1,300 - 1,600
MS-60:	$1,800 - 2,200
MS-63:	$17,000 - 21,000

CONDITION CENSUS:

To qualify at the Condition Census level, an 1875 Double Eagle must grade at least Mint State-63.

NOTES

1875-CC

MINTAGE: 111,151
RARITY RANKINGS:
   Overall: 27th of 31   **By Mint:** 6th of 7
   Premium Quality: 27th of 31   **By Mint:** 7th of 7

     The 1875-CC is the second most common Double Eagle from the Carson City Mint. It is also one of the two or three most common Double Eagles struck at this mint. It appears that a significant percentage of the original mintage probably never entered circulation as evidenced by the large number of high grade pieces which exist today.

     The quality of strike found on examples of this date varies. While some coins are found with sharply detailed obverse stars, many coins show flatness on the radial lines. The hair of Liberty is usually rather soft although some pieces do show decent definition in this area. The edges are somewhat rounded and have an almost bevelled appearance. The reverse is generally sharp. The luster on 1875-CC Double Eagles is excellent. Many pieces have very heavily marked surfaces and there are numerous 1875-CC Double Eagles which are technically "Uncirculated" but which are given About Uncirculated grades by PCGS and NGC because these abrasions give the appearance of wear. Pieces are known which are fully Prooflike (these are scarce) while others have superb rich mint frost. The coloration ranges from intense yellow-gold to green-gold or even coppery orange. It is not uncommon to find examples which have mint-made copper spots on the surfaces. If these spots are not too severe, they do not affect the value of a coin.

At least two die varieties are known. On the first, the mintmark is very closely spaced. On the second, it is wider. It is unknown which of these two is scarcer.

The 1875-CC Double Eagle is a very popular coin. Its availability in higher grades makes it an excellent coin for a type collector. Lower grade examples can be purchased for a very small premium over common date value. In the lower Mint State grades this is a reasonably common issue. It becomes rare in MS-63.

RARITY:
Total Known: 2500-3000+
Overall Rarity By Grade:

VF	EF	AU	MINT STATE
250-350	800-900	1000-1200	450-550

PRICE LEVELS:

AU-50:	$2,200 - 2,600
MS-60:	$4,800 - 6,000
MS-63:	$35,000 - 40,000

CONDITION CENSUS:

An 1875-CC Double Eagle which grades Mint State-63 qualifies as a Condition Census example of this date.

1875-S

MINTAGE: 1,230,000
RARITY RANKINGS:
   Overall: 29th of 31   **By Mint:** 11th of 12
   Premium Quality: 29th of 31   **By Mint:** 11th of 12

The 1875-S has the second highest mintage figure of any Type Two Double Eagle. It is one of the more common issues of this type, both in terms of its overall rarity and in premium quality grades. After the 1876-S, it is the most common Type Two Double Eagle struck at the San Francisco Mint.

1875-S Double Eagles show a slightly better strike than some of the earlier issues from this mint. While many coins show characteristic flatness on the hair of Liberty, it is possible to find an example which show a decent amount of intricate detail. The reverse is generally well struck with most pieces showing good detail on the feathers and wing tips of the eagle. The surfaces on the typical 1875-S Double Eagle are heavily abraded with deep, detracting marks visible in the fields. Some pieces display Mint-made faults such as black grease stains or copper spots. If these marks are unobtrusive, they are not considered detracting by the grading services. The luster on this issue is very good. High grade, uncleaned 1875-S Double Eagles show rich Mint frost which can be very appealing if the surfaces show fewer bagmarks than normal. The coloration on original examples tends to run towards rose-gold, orange-gold or other fairly light shades. It is sometimes possible to find an example of this date with good eye appeal but most pieces are unappealing. Coins with minimal marks, good luster and nice color invariably realize premium prices when they are sold.

A number of die varieties exist but these remain mostly unexplored. They typically entail the size and placement of the mintmark.

The 1875-S Double Eagle is very common in lower grades and it can be located without much effort in Mint State-60. This date is very scarce in Mint State-62 and it becomes very rare in Mint State-63. It is extremely rare in any grade higher than this. The finest known example of this date is a spectacular NGC MS-67 which was earlier sold in a 1995 auction sale. It was being offered for sale for over $200,000. This coin is one of the finest business strike Type Two Double Eagles of any date which is currently known to exist.

RARITY:
Total Known: 2950-3250
Overall Rarity By Grade:

VF	EF	AU	MINT STATE
100-150	450-500	1700-1800	700-800

PRICE LEVELS:

AU-50:	$1,300 - 1,600
MS-60:	$1,800 - 2,200
MS-63:	$23,000 - 27,000

CONDITION CENSUS:

An 1875-S Double Eagle which grades Mint State-62 qualifies as Condition Census for this issue.

NOTES

1876

MINTAGE: 583,905
RARITY RANKINGS:
   Overall: 25th of 31   **By Mint:** 11th of 12
   Premium Quality: 28th of 31   **By Mint:** 11th of 12

    The 1876 is the final Type Two Double Eagle produced at the Philadelphia Mint. It is among the most common dates of this type and it is generally among the first issues which a specialist will acquire when putting together a date set. This date has always been popular due to its having been issued during the centennial year.

    Most 1876 Double Eagles show a relatively good quality of strike. On most pieces, the hair of Liberty is not fully defined but some pieces do show better than average detail. The stars are often full with the radial lines complete. On the reverse, the wings and feathers of the eagle are better defined than on earlier Type Two issues from the Philadelphia Mint. The typical 1876 Double Eagle shows numerous deep, detracting marks on the surfaces. The luster on higher grade, original pieces is very good. Many examples show frosty mint luster while a few are semi-Prooflike with partially to nearly fully reflective fields. Uncleaned, high grade 1876 Double Eagles have green-gold, orange-gold or light rose coloration. It is not impossible to locate an example of this date which has above-average eye appeal. However, many coins are somewhat unappealing due to overly bagmarked surfaces and impaired luster.

No significant die varieties are known although it is probable that a number of minor varieties exist.

45 Proofs were struck. Approximately a dozen survive and these are seldom seen except at important auction sales.

The 1876 Double Eagle is common in circulated grades and in the lower Mint State grades as well. It becomes scarce in MS-62, rare in MS-63 and it is very rare in any grade higher than this.

RARITY:
Total Known: 1700-2000+
Overall Rarity By Grade:

VF	EF	AU	MINT STATE
50-75	50-75	1000-1200	600-700

PRICE LEVELS:

AU-50:	$1,30 - 1,600
MS-60:	$1,800 - 2,200
MS-63:	$23,000 - 27,000

CONDITION CENSUS:

An 1876 Double Eagle must grade at least Mint State-63 (and be choice for the grade) in order to qualify as a Condition Census example.

NOTES

1876-CC

MINTAGE: 138,441
RARITY RANKINGS:
   Overall: 28th of 31   **By Mint:** 7th of 7
   Premium Quality: 26th of 31   **By Mint:** 6th of 7

    More Double Eagles were struck at the Carson City mint in 1876 than in any other year during this Mint's existence (1870-1893). The 1876-CC is the most common Type Two Carson City Double Eagle from the standpoint of overall rarity.

    Examples of this date are often found with weakness of strike on some of the obverse stars and on the hair of Liberty. The reverse shows sharp detail and appears crisper than the obverse. 1876-CC Double Eagles generally have good luster which can range from Prooflike to satiny to slightly dull. The colorations most often seen are bright yellow gold and greenish-gold. Pieces are sometimes found with copper spots and these are not considered detracting unless they are very heavy or conspicuously located. The surfaces on many examples of this date are very heavily abraded and this is a hard date to locate with good eye appeal.

    Varieties exist with the mintmark spaced closely and with the mintmark showing more distance between the two C's.

The 1876-CC Double Eagle has become relatively easy to obtain in all circulated grades up to and including AU-55. Until recently, this date was very rare in any Uncirculated grade. In fact, the first 1876-CC Double Eagle to have ever been graded Mint State-61 by PCGS realized close to $14,000 in a January, 1993 auction. Since then, at least two groups of Uncirculated coins have been uncovered and well distributed into numismatic channels. The 1876-CC can be elusive in MS-61 and remains a very rare coin in MS-62.

RARITY:
Total Known: 2800-3300
Overall Rarity By Grade:

VF	EF	AU	MINT STATE
250-350	1100-1250	1250-1400	200-250

PRICE LEVELS:

AU-50:	$2,500 - 3,000
MS-60:	$8,000 - 10,000
MS-63:	$50,000 - 60,000

CONDITION CENSUS:

A Condition Census 1876-CC Double Eagle will grade Mint State-62 and be choice for the grade.

NOTES

1876-S

MINTAGE: 1,597,000
RARITY RANKINGS:
   Overall: 30th of 31   **By Mint:** 12th of 12
   Premium Quality: 30th of 31   **By Mint:** 12th of 12

The 1876-S is the final issue in the Type Two Double Eagle series. It has the second highest mintage figure of any date in this series and it is the second most common coin.

The 1876-S has a quality of strike which is very similar to that seen on the 1875-S. Some examples are known which show very good strikes; others have strikes which show weakness on the hair of Liberty like so many Type Two Double Eagles do. The surfaces on many examples of this date are heavily abraded with deep marks visible in the obverse fields and on the cheek of Liberty. The luster ranges from satiny to frosty with a few semi-Prooflike pieces known. The coloration on high grade, uncleaned ranges from rose-gold to deep orange. It is possible to locate examples with above-average eye appeal. This makes the 1876-S Double Eagle a very popular coin with type collectors as it is inexpensive in the lower Mint State grades and pleasing pieces are available.

There are no significant die varieties currently recorded but it is probable that many mintmark positions exist.

The 1876-S Double Eagle is very common in all circulated grades. In the lower Mint State grades it is very easy to locate as well. This date is fairly scarce in Mint State-62 and it becomes rare in MS-63. A few lovely MS-64's exist; these are very rare and extremely desirable.

RARITY:
Total Known: 3300-4100+
Overall Rarity By Grade:

VF	EF	AU	MINT STATE
50-75	250-325	1500-2000	1500-1700

PRICE LEVELS:

AU-50:	$1,300 - 1,600
MS-60:	$1,800 - 2,200
MS-63:	$16,000 - 20,000

CONDITION CENSUS:

An 1876-S Double Eagle which grades Mint State-63 is regarded as a Condition Census example of this date.

NOTES

OVERALL RARITY ALL MINTS

This chart refers to the rarity of all Type Two Double Eagles in terms of their overall rarity—i.e., how many examples of each date exist in all grades combined

1.	1870-CC	17.	1874
2.	1871-CC	18.	1872-S
3.	1868	19.	1871-S
4.	1870	20.	1868-S
5.	1872-CC	21.	1875
6.	1873 Closed 3	22.	1869-S
7.	1871	23.	1873-S Closed 3
8.	1873-S Open 3	24.	1874-S
9.	1873-CC	25.	1876
10.	1869	26.	1874-CC
11.	1867	27.	1875-CC
12.	1866	28.	1876-CC
13.	1867-S	29.	1875-S
14.	1866-S With Motto	30.	1876-S
15.	1870-S	31.	1873 Open 3
16.	1872		

PREMIUM QUALITY RARITY - ALL MINTS

This chart refers to the rarity of each Type Two Double Eagle in "premium grades" - i.e., About Uncirculated-55 and better

1.	1870-CC	17.	1872
2.	1871-CC	18.	1874
3.	1868	19.	1871-S
4.	1872-CC	20.	1872-S
5.	1870	21.	1869-S
6.	1871	22.	1874-CC
7.	1873-CC	23.	1873-S Closed 3
8.	1873 Closed 3	24.	1875
9.	1873-S Open 3	25.	1874-S
10.	1869	26.	1876-CC
11.	1867-S	27.	1875-CC
12.	1866-S With Motto	28.	1876
13.	1866	29.	1875-S
14.	1870-S	30.	1876-S
15.	1867	31.	1873 Open 3
16.	1868-S		

OVERALL RARITY PHILADELPHIA MINT

This chart ranks the overall rarity—from rarest to most common— of each Type Two Double Eagle struck at the Philadelphia Mint.

1. 1868

2. 1870

3. 1873 Closed 3

4. 1871

5. 1869

6. 1867

7. 1866

8. 1874

9. 1872

10. 1875

11. 1876

12. 1873 Open 3

PREMIUM QUALITY RARITY PHILADELPHIA MINT

"Premium Quality" refers to all coins of a specific issue which grade About Uncirculated-55 or better. This chart ranks each Philadelphia Type two Double Eagle in the Premium Quality grades

1. 1868

2. 1870

3. 1871

4. 1873 Closed 3

5. 1869

6. 1866

7. 1867

8. 1872

9. 1874

10. 1875

11. 1876

12. 1873 Open 3

OVERALL RARITY
SAN FRANCISCO MINT

1. 1873-S Open 3

2. 1867-S

3. 1866-S With Motto

4. 1870-S

5. 1872-S

6. 1871-S

7. 1868-S

8. 1869-S

9. 1873-S Closed 3

10. 1874-S

11. 1875-S

12. 1876-S

PREMIUM QUALITY RARITY SAN FRANCISCO MINT

1. 1873-S Open 3

2. 1867-S

3. 1866-S With Motto

4. 1870-S

5. 1868-S

6. 1871-S

7. 1872-S

8. 1869-S

9. 1873-S Closed 3

10. 1874-S

11. 1875-S

12. 1876-S

OVERALL RARITY CARSON CITY MINT (Type Two Only)

1.   1870-CC
2.   1871-CC
3.   1872-CC
4.   1873-CC
5.   1874-CC
6.   1875-CC
7.   1876-CC

PREMIUM QUALITY RARITY CARSON CITY MINT (Type Two Only)

1.   1870-CC
2.   1871-CC
3.   1872-CC
4.   1873-CC
5.   1874-CC
6.   1876-CC
7.   1875-CC

OVERALL RARITY CARSON CITY MINT (ALL TYPES)

1. 1870-CC
2. 1891-CC
3. 1871-CC
4. 1879-CC
5. 1878-CC
6. 1885-CC
7. 1872-CC
8. 1873-CC
9. 1877-CC
10. 1893-CC
11. 1892-CC
12. 1882-CC
13. 1889-CC
14. 1883-CC
15. 1884-CC
16. 1890-CC
17. 1874-CC
18. 1876-CC
19. 1875-CC

PREMIUM QUALITY - RARITY CARSON MINT (ALL TYPES)

1. 1870-CC
2. 1879-CC
3. 1871-CC
4. 1878-CC
5. 1891-CC
6. 1872-CC
7. 1885-CC
8. 1877-CC
9. 1873-CC
10. 1882-CC
11. 1892-CC
12. 1883-CC
13. 1893-CC
14. 1884-CC
15. 1889-CC
16. 1890-CC
17. 1874-CC
18. 1876-CC
19. 1875-CC

GLOSSARY

The following terms appear throughout this book. For the sake of the collector who is not familiar with them, these terms are defined in this section.

Abrasion: A mark on a coin caused by contact with another coin.

Bagmark: A mark on a coin caused by contact with other coins when placed inside a bag for shipment to a bank. Most Type Two Double Eagles, like all large-sized gold coins, show extensive bagmarks from this process.

Border: A design element employing a raised circle with the outer circumference called the rim. On Type Two Double Eagles, the border consists of beads.

Business Strike: A coin which was struck for general circulation. Business strikes were intended to be used in the normal course of commerce.

Clashmarks: Impressions of a portion of the detail of one side of a coin onto another in the field of a die facing it. These occur when dies strike each other during the coinage process without a planchet or blank between them.

Closed 3: The style of the numeral 3 found on the earliest dies of the Philadelphia and San Francisco Double Eagles dated 1873. On these dies, the knobs of the 3 are so close together that they could be mistaken for an 8.

Comparative Rarity: The relative rarity of a specific issue in a specific grade when compared to another issue in the same grade.

Condition Census: A ranking of the 10 to 15 finest known examples of a specific issue, including ties.

Die: A piece of fabricated steel which stamps the design into a planchet.

Die Variety: Distinct varieties within a specific issue caused by using or combining new dies within a coinage run.

Edge: The cylindrical boundary of a coin.

Edge Reeding: Raised ribs on the edge of a coin which serve as an anti-counterfeiting device. All Liberty Head Double Eagles have a reeded edge.

Eye Appeal: A combination of characteristics such as luster, strike and coloration which make a coin, literally, appealing to the eye.

Grade: The rating of a coin's place on a numerical scale which encompasses the range between extreme wear and perfection.

Hairlines: Fine scratches which are caused by cleaning a coin with an abrasive.

Hoard: A group of coins, which can vary greatly in size, which have been taken off the market by a non-numismatic source and which re-enters the market through a numismatic source. A hoard may contain one specific date or many dates. When a hoard contains multiple examples of one date, this issue may possibly lose value but other dates which share its design may gain value through increased collector demand.

Key Date: A date in a series which is often popular and recognized as an especially difficult date to locate in all grades. The key date in the Type Two Double Eagle series is the 1870-CC.

Mint State: A coin with no wear. Mint State coins are rated on a scale which goes from Mint State-60 to Mint State-70.

NGC: Numismatic Guaranty Corporation, a New Jersey-based third party grader and authenticator of coins.

Obverse: The front or the face side of a coin.

Open 3: The style of 3 found on the later dies of the Philadelphia and San Francisco Double Eagle dies of 1873.

Overall Rarity: A term which refers to the total number of examples known of a specific issue.

PCGS: The Professional Coin Grading Service, a California-based third party grader and authenticator of coins.

Pedigree: The chain of ownership of a coin or a collection. A coin pedigreed to a famous collection typically carries a premium over a non-pedigreed coin.

Population Report: A listing published by both NGC and PCGS which lists the number of coins graded and how the individual coins break down. Each date in the Type Two Double Eagle series is listed in both services reports.

Premium Quality: Within the parameters of this book, the term Premium Quality refers to coins which grade About Uncirculated-55 or higher.

Proof: A coin which is struck specially for collectors on a polished planchet. Proof coins receive multiple blows of the dies and are afforded special care and handling.

Prooflike: A coin struck for circulation which has some of the reflective qualities of a Proof coin. Type Two Double Eagles which are Prooflike can sell for substantial premiums.

Reverse: The back side of a coin.

Set Premium: At times in some markets, a complete set of coins is worth more than the sum of the individual pieces it contains. This is known as a set premium by numismatists.

Sleeper: A coin which is underrated and undervalued is said to be a sleeper. In the Type Two Double Eagle series, the 1874 is currently regarded as a sleeper.

Transitional Issue: A coin on which the design on one side is current and which the other side has a design which is later adopted. In the Type Two Double Eagle series, the 1866-S is a Transitional Issue as it exists both with and without the motto IN GOD WE TRUST.

Type One Double Eagle: A United States twenty dollar gold piece struck at either the Philadelphia, New Orleans or San Francisco mints between 1850 and 1866. This type is most easily identifiable by the absence of the motto IN GOD WE TRUST on the reverse.

Type Two Double Eagle: A United States twenty dollar gold piece struck at either the Philadelphia, Carson City or San Francisco mints between 1866 and 1876. This type is most identifiable by the presence of the motto IN GOD WE TRUST on the reverse and the value denoted as TWENTY D.

Type Three Double Eagle: A United States twenty dollar gold piece struck at either the Philadelphia, New Orleans, Carson City, San Francisco or Denver mints between1877 and 1907. This type is most identifiable by the value denoted as TWENTY DOLLARS.

Weak Strike: A coin which shows inferior detail as a result of the striking process. A weakly struck coin is only accorded a reduced value if most examples of the specific date in question are well struck.

Well Struck: A coin which shows good detail as the result of the striking process. A well struck coin is accorded high value if most examples of the specific date in question are weakly struck.

Uncirculated: A coin with no wear. See Mint State.

Type Two Double Eagle Checklist

DATE	GRADE/SERVICE	DATE ACQUIRED	PRICE PAID
1866			
1866-S			
1867			
1867-S			
1868			
1868-S			
1869			
1869-S			
1870			
1870-CC			
1870-S			
1871			
1871-CC			

DATE	GRADE/SERVICE	DATE ACQUIRED	PRICE PAID
1871-S			
1872			
1872-CC			
1872-S			
1873 Closed 3			
1873 Open 3			
1873-CC			
1873-S Open 3			
1873-S Closed 3			
1874			
1874-CC			
1874-S			
1875			
1875-CC			
1875-S			

1876

1876-CC

1876-S

EXTRA COINS:

NOTES: